No Dogs Allowed
Buffy the Cat

BY PAUL SMULSON

Revised Edition

Published by Graphix Products, Inc.
399 Wegner Drive
West Chicago, IL 60185

Printed in China

ISBN 978-0-9749989-4-7

Library of Congress Control Number: 2009931673

My entire life, I was not a cat fan. When I went to my friends' homes who had cats, I kept my distance. Then in 1994, my wife and I went to the home of my neighbor and friend, George Ireland, the coach of the Loyola Ramblers. He said, "Robin, Paul, come downstairs and see what I have for your daughters." There were two kittens sitting in front of us. I looked at Robin immediately with a decision to make. I did not want the kittens, but how could I say no to the Coach? George sat in his recliner and introduced us to Buffy and Smokey. Robin said, "Gabbi and Randi will love the cats."

Buffy jumped on George's lap and George began to pet his stomach. At that point he said, "Someday, Paul, you will be doing this." I looked at Robin with a look that she knew meant, "I don't think so."

I would like to dedicate this book to George Ireland, coach of the Loyola University 1963 NCAA Basketball Champions.

Foreword

One day, we found Buffy keeping to himself in the corner of the basement. He refused to eat and appeared to be sick. We took him to the vet, who informed us that Buffy was a very sick cat. The diagnosis was lymphoma, but they needed to complete a few more tests to be sure. Surgery would cost 800 dollars. This would determine if Buffy had lymphoma or stone blockage in the kidney.

My daughter, Gabbi, and I took pictures of Buffy and called it *Buffy's Last Roll.* We went to the veterinary hospital to drop off Buffy in the waiting room. Another pet owner asked Gabbi, who was holding Buffy, "What is wrong with your cat?"

Gabbi responded sadly, "He might have lymphoma." Buffy was taken to the back of the animal hospital and we went home.

A few days later, the doctor called and told

uffy starts his day

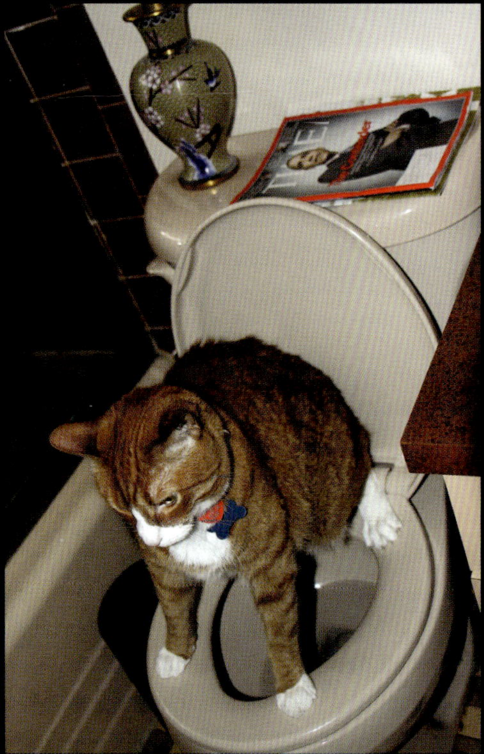

Freezer
Feline
c/d
Feline
c/d

NO PULP
CALCIUM
PURE PREMIUM
100%
PURE ORANGE JUICE
CALCIUM & VITAMIN D

Profile

OATMEAL STOUT
12 FL OZ (355 ML)

Definitely a beer man

Celebrating

TRY
TRASH
3

ICE CREAM & COLD
3
Hey Man! Watch for children!

Shopping

Fancy Feast
IAMS
Eukanuba

Bernie Mac
remembered
Gold standard

Smartest cat in the class

MULTIVARIABLE
CALCULUS

$z = \sqrt{x^2+y^2}$ Find $\frac{\partial^2 z}{\partial x^2}$
$\frac{\partial z}{\partial x} = \frac{1}{2}(x^2+y^2)^{-1/2} 2x$
$= \frac{x}{\sqrt{x^2+y^2}}$
$\frac{\partial^2 z}{\partial x^2} = x\left(-\frac{1}{2}\right)(x^2+y^2)^{-3/2}(2x) + (x^2+y^2)^{-1/2}$
$= \frac{y^2}{(x^2+y^2)^{3/2}}$

Activities

4
5
WILMETTE

MERCURY

HOBIE CAT

NON CONDUCTIVE
FIBERGLASS

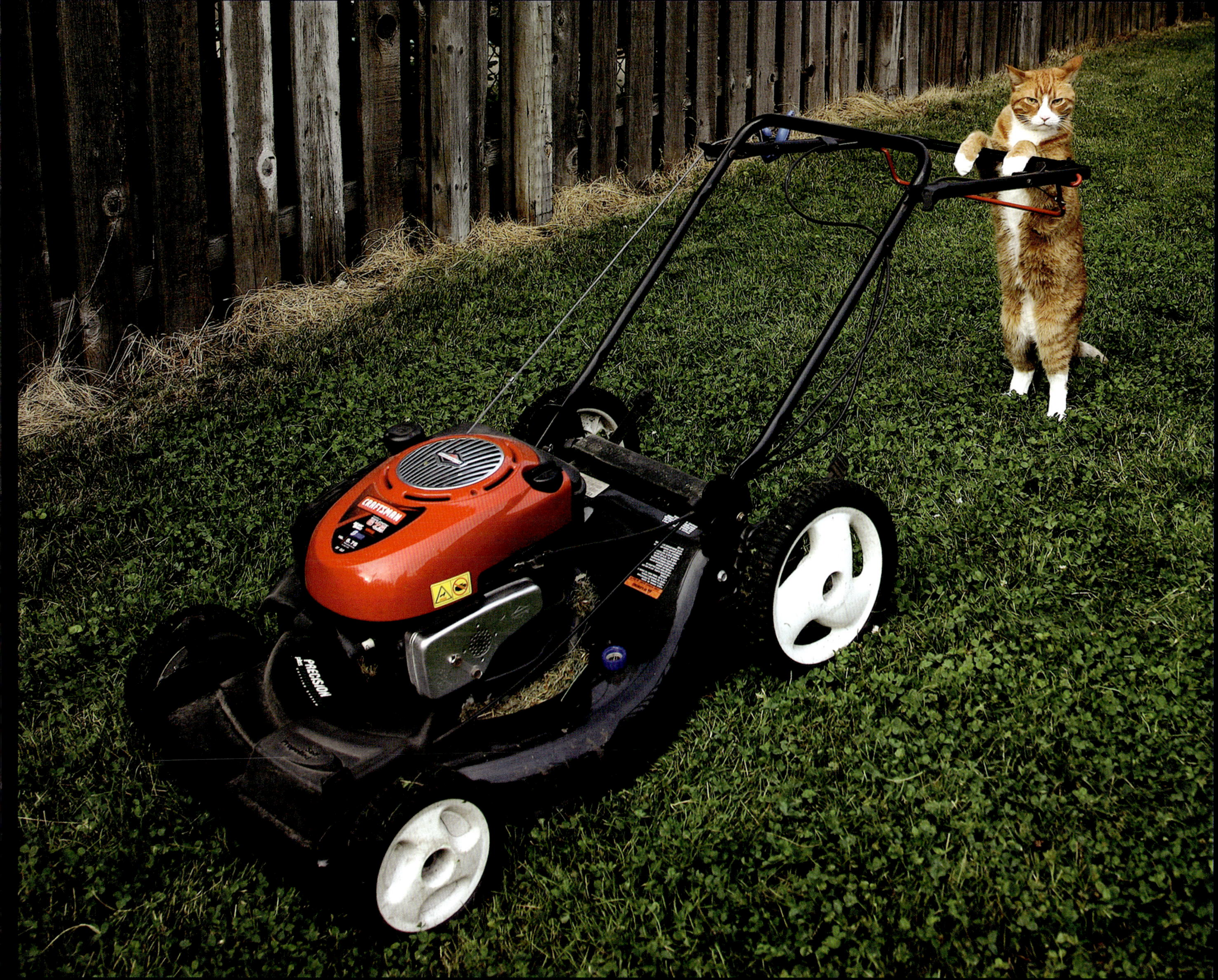
CRAFTSMAN
PRECISION

España

NORMAN ROCKWELL
NORMAN ROCKWELL

PALM &
TAROT CARDS

LOW IMPACT
TREADMILL

ULL
Official Game Ball

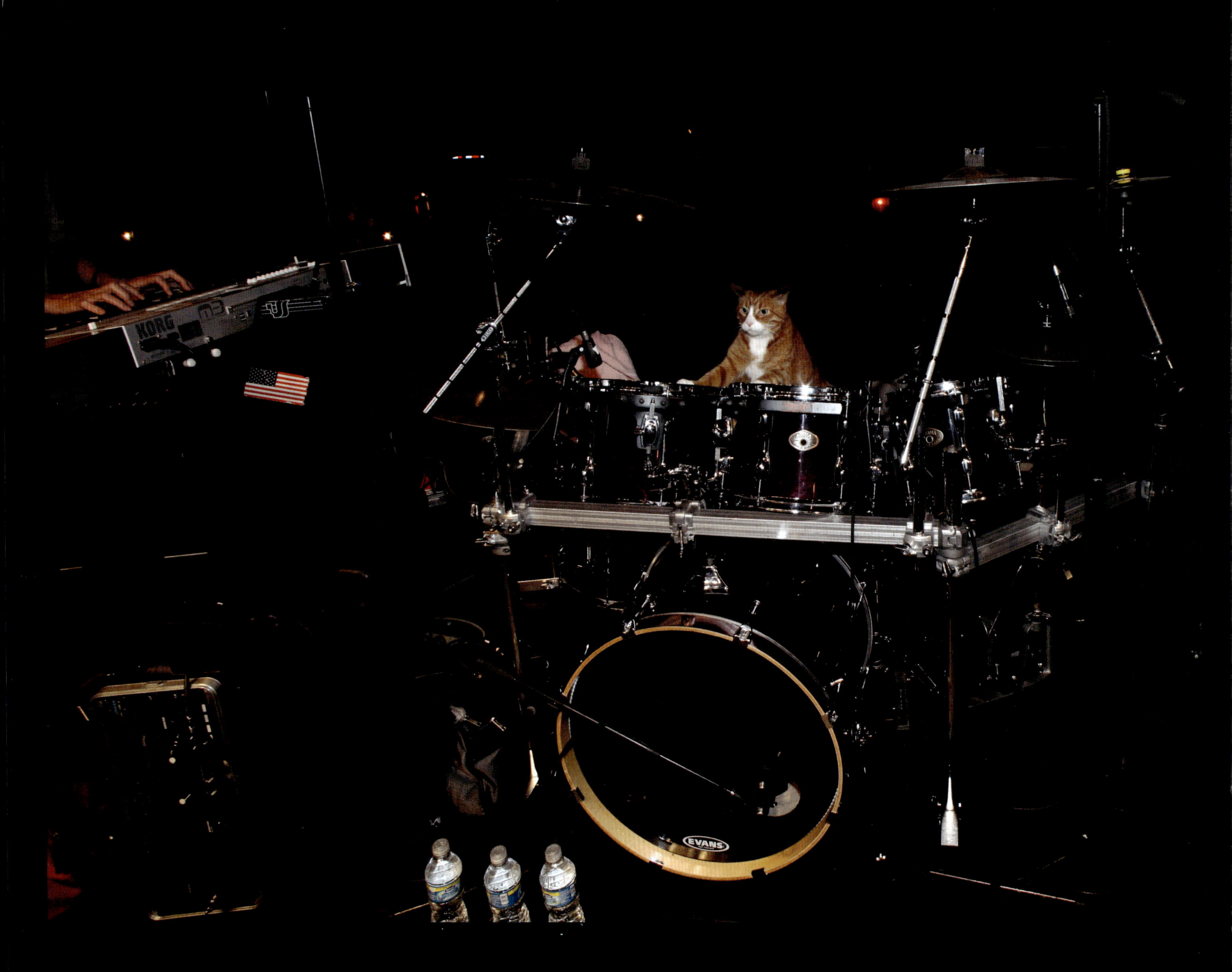
KORG
EVANS

Responsibilities

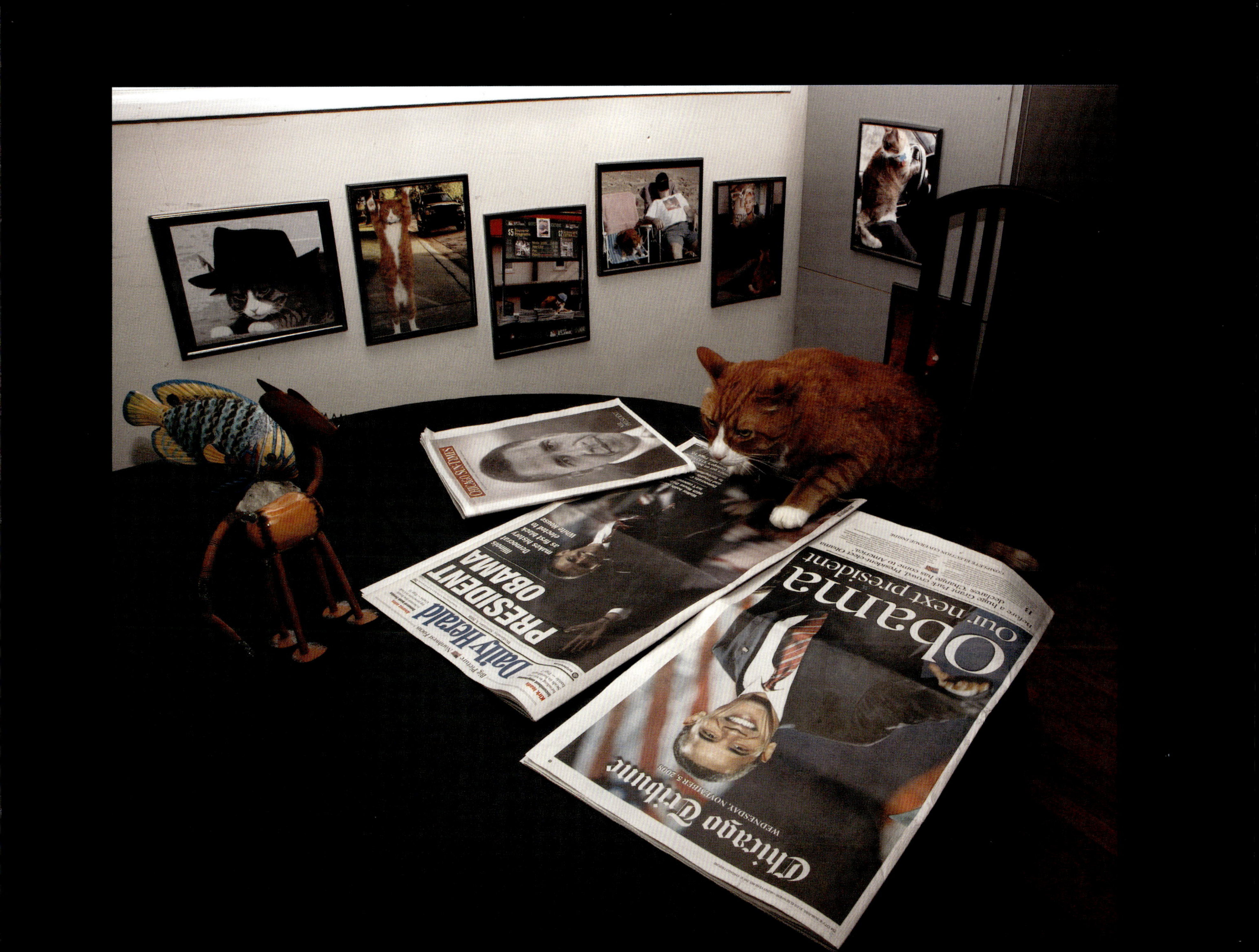

Chicago Tribune
WEDNESDAY, NOVEMBER 5, 2008
Obama
Our next president
Daily Herald
PRESIDENT OBAMA
Illinois Democrat makes history as first black elected to White House

Entertainment

Skokie
8800N
5000W

3458
cta

Members,
Ticket Holders, Will Call

CENTER
MICHAEL JORDAN

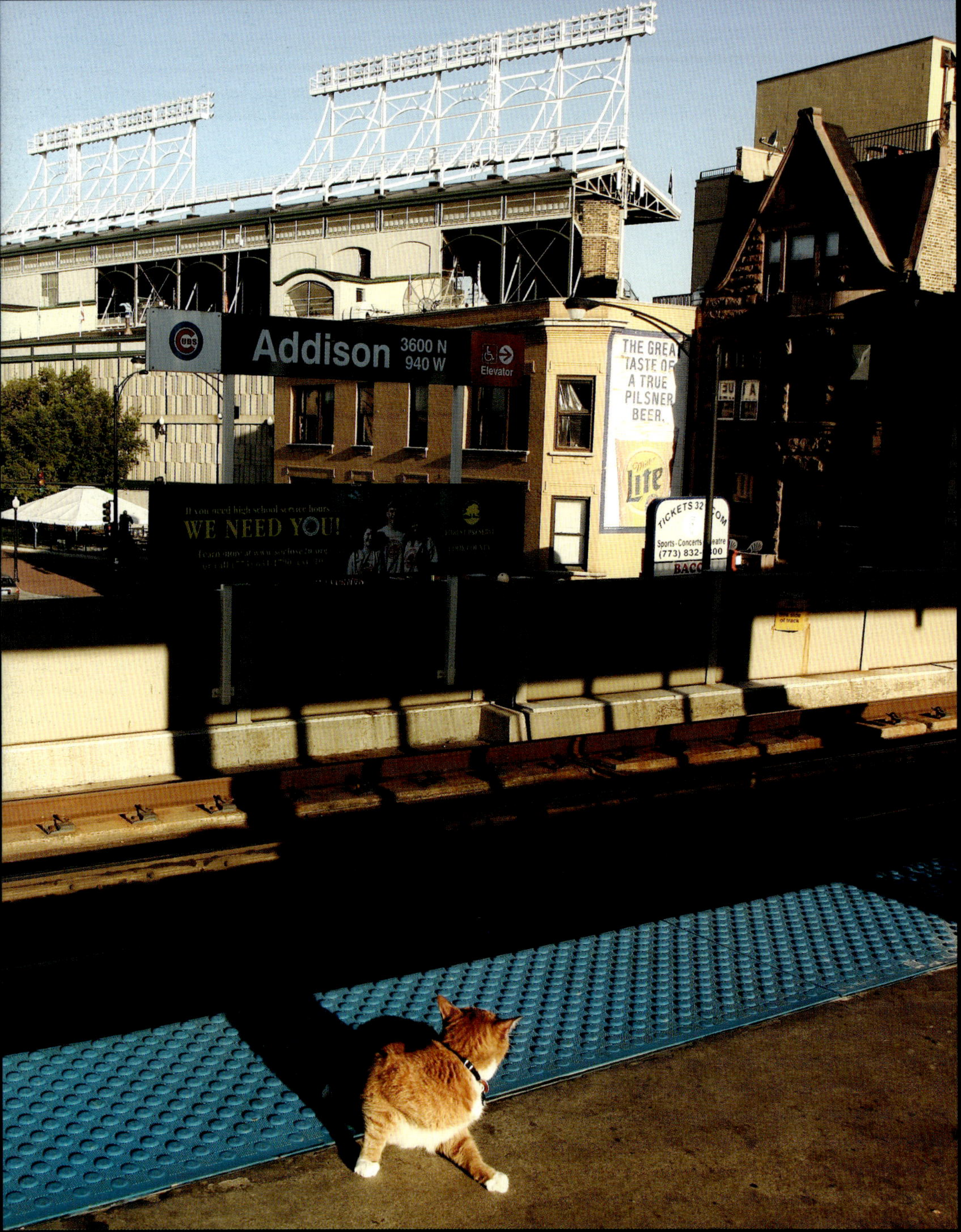
Addison
3600 N
940 W
Elevator
THE GREAT
TASTE OF
A TRUE
PILSNER
BEER.
Lite
WE NEED YOU!

WRIGLEY FIELD
HOME OF
CHICAGO CUBS
WELCOME TO
WRIGLEY FIELD
Ticket
Services
Pass
Window
G
NOTICE
12
11
10
CLOSED
CLOSED
CLOSED

"LET ME HEAR 'YA ...
A ONE ... A TWO ... A THREE ....."
- HARRY CARAY

I Live for This
NEW
2008 YEARBOOK
$15
$5 Souvenir Programs
CUBS2008
$2 Scorecard EXTRA FREE PENCIL
SCORECARD
Media Guide $15.00
Vine Line $3.00
Pen .50¢
Pencil Free w/scorecard .25¢
G
CLOSED
No Smoking in Wrigley Field
OFFICIAL PUBLICATIONS
I Live for This
OFFICIAL

78
CHICAGO FIRE DEPT.
FDD597
CUBS

Lager
Haus Lager

CASH

Tailgating

TRESPASS

Transportation

SAFETY

NISSAN

LEARN TO
FLY HERE!

STEP
BELOW

APU CONTROL
ERASE TEST
STATUS
HEADPHONE
ELECTRICAL
FUEL
POWERPLANT
FLIGHT CONTROLS
HYDRAULIC
PULL TO SHUTOFF
ROTATE TO EXTG
ERJ 145
GO AROUND
GO AROUND
FLAP

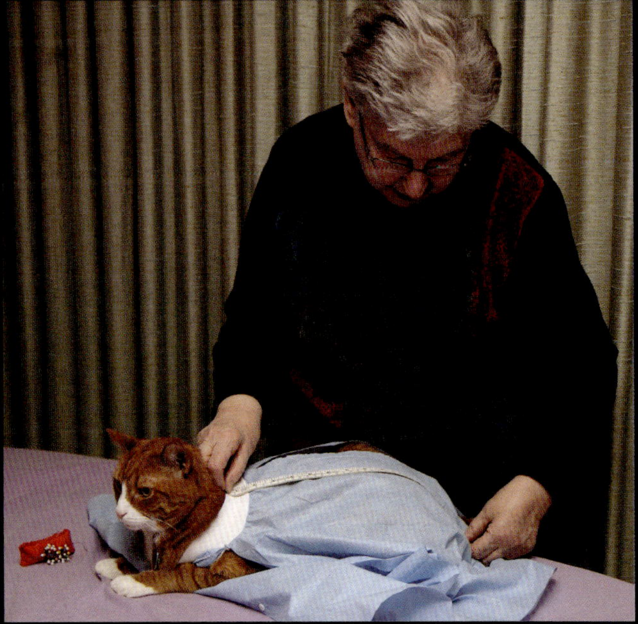

Professional careers

DENTIST

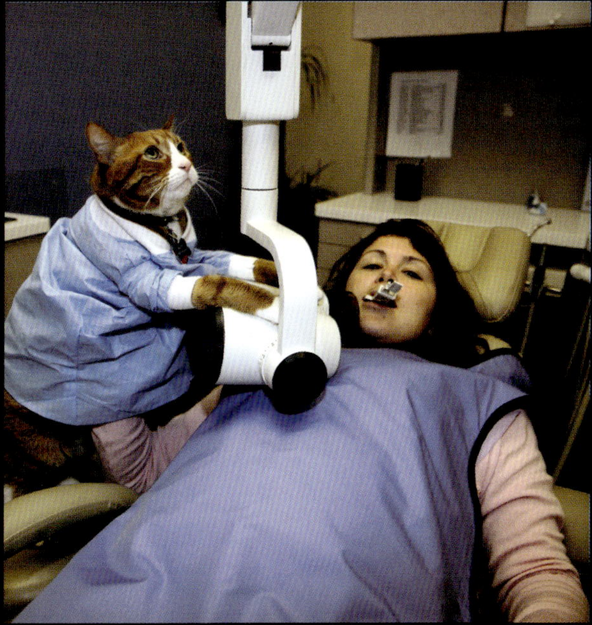

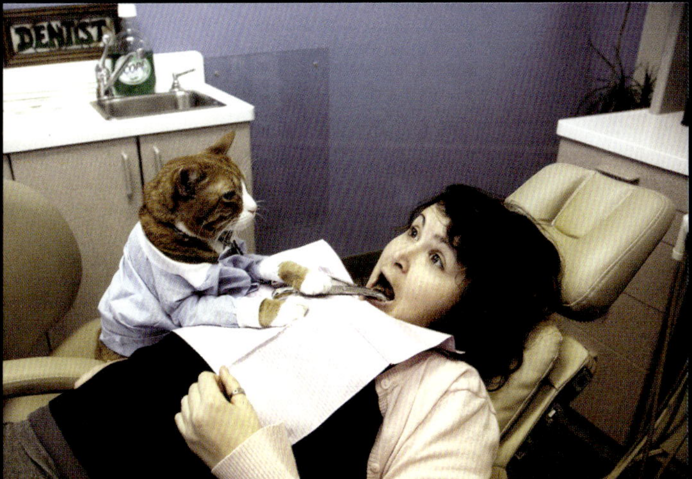
DENTIST

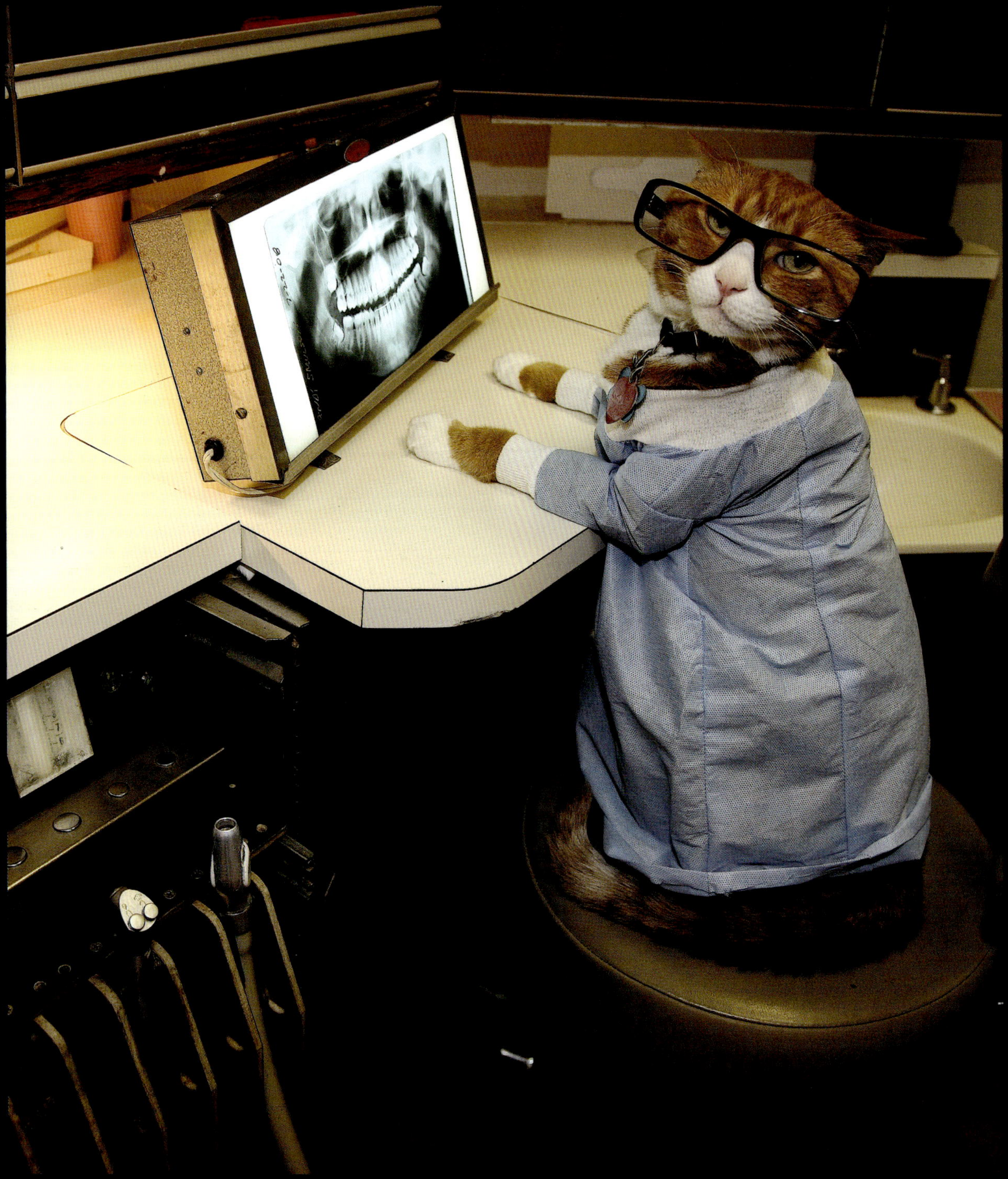

SEAL OF COOK COUNTY
ILLINOIS
JANUARY 1831

COUNTY
ILLINOIS
JANUARY 1831
Black's Law Dictionary

SONY
SWIDERSKI

Model 309A
MADE IN U.S.A.

PURA VIDA
COSTA RICA

NO DOGS

Relaxing by the fire

la notte
quieta sopra e
e in
agli
la luna
la notte
chiara é
lento e
i tetti

Retirement life

kibitz
kibbitz
kibitzer
kibbitzer

NO
DOGS
ALLOWED